CHUCK CLOSE

LIFE AND WORK
1988-1995

TEXT BY JOHN GUARE

THAMES AND HUDSON
IN ASSOCIATION WITH
YARROW PRESS

Any copy of this book issued by the publisher
is sold subject to the condition that it shall
not by way of trade or otherwise be lent,
resold, hired out, or otherwise circulated
without the publisher's prior consent in any
form of binding or cover other than that in
which it is published, and without a similar
condition including these words being imposed
on a subsequent purchaser.

First published in the United States of America
in hardcover in 1995
by Thames and Hudson Inc., 500 Fifth Avenue,
New York, New York 10110

First published in Great Britain in 1995
by Thames and Hudson Ltd, London

This book was conceived by Anne Yarowsky
and produced by Yarrow Press, New York.

Library of Congress Catalog Card Number 95-60602

British Library Cataloguing-in-Publishing Data
A catalogue record for this book is available
from the British Library

ISBN 0-500-09253-2

Designed by Chip Kidd

Printed and bound in Singapore

Front endpaper painting and details following:
Chuck Close. SELF-PORTRAIT. 1991.
OIL ON CANVAS, 100 X 84".
COLLECTION PAINEWEBBER GROUP, INC., NEW YORK

Half-title spread paintings:
Left page: Chuck Close. JOHN (in progress). 1992.
Right page: Chuck Close. JOHN. 1992.
OIL ON CANVAS, 100 X 84".
COLLECTION MICHAEL AND JUDY OVITZ, LOS ANGELES

CONTENTS

PORTRAIT OF THE
ARTIST

BY JOHN GUARE

The great faces Chuck Close paints remind me of the statues found on Easter Island.

Leslie

What were they there for? Were these the gods? Why their great size? I easily imagine myself an archaeologist centuries from now digging miles down through the rubble of an ancient city called New York and coming upon a number of 7-by-9-foot paintings of people named Fanny and painted by someone who must be an official court painter named Chuck Close. As an archaeologist I would surmise, "Aha, in this twentieth-century civilization, these subjects must have been the gods, the rulers, the most famous people of that ancient time."

But Chuck Close could never be called an official painter. His subjects are hardly the stuff of celebrity. They're his friends, his relatives. He is, however, a seminal figure in contemporary American art. In 1980-81, which was his fortieth year, he had a major retrospective copresented by the Walker Art Museum in Minneapolis and the Whitney Museum of American Art in New York. By 1988, Chuck Close's work had been the subject of sixty solo shows and been represented in hundreds of group shows around the world. By 1988, Chuck Close was at a rare point in any artist's career. No one could begrudge him his success. The work was too original and too good. In October 1988, he showed his new paintings at Pace Gallery in New York. The work was looser, freer. Chuck was painting painters: Cindy Sherman, Francesco Clemente, Lucas Samaras. Perhaps that accounted for the sense of change.

Then, a few weeks after that show in late 1988, news spread like a toxic oil spill that a mysterious catastrophe had stricken Chuck Close, leaving him totally destroyed. Was he going to live? Perhaps yes, for now, went the word. But he'll never paint again. A career is ended? "Absolutely," clucked the experts. "Only Memory Lane retrospectives for Chuck Close from now on."

In the years immediately after that catastrophe, I would come upon one of Close's enormous portraits in the permanent collections of the Whitney or the Metropolitan Museum of Art or MoMA or the National Gallery of Art and be stunned by their purity. They hung there like great passport photos.

PRECEDING PAGES:
Page 16
STONE AGE STATUE (detail),
EASTER ISLAND.

Page 17
Chuck Close. BIG SELF-PORTRAIT (detail). 1968.
ACRYLIC ON CANVAS, 107 1/2 X 83 1/2".
WALKER ART CENTER, MINNEAPOLIS. ART CENTER
ACQUISITION FUND, 1969

Chuck Close. LESLIE. 1973.
WATERCOLOR ON PAPER, 72 1/2 X 57".
PRIVATE COLLECTION

But passports to what country? This is the great mystery of his work. Passports are used on a journey. But what was the nature of Close's journey? We'd never know the answer. Like John Lennon or George Gershwin or Jackson Pollock or F. Scott Fitzgerald, Close was another artist snatched away before his immense talent was fully explored.

And then, at the end of 1991, a notice appeared in the papers announcing very matter of factly that a show of new paintings by Chuck Close would open on November 2, 1991, at the Pace Gallery in SoHo. New paintings? Chuck's still alive? Oh no—the work of the disabled. Charity will be demanded. If Chuck's there, say, "Good work, old boy. Keep up the good work. So brave. Where can I send a donation? Is there a telethon for what you have?"

I went downtown to Greene Street. The new work made me gasp. The paintings were still on the same large scale. The landscape was still the human face staring out at you, but all cool objectivity was gone. I remember reeling around the gallery trying to take them all in. Look at the portrait of April. How did Close find Monet's dazzling garden in Giverny in April's face? Look at the rage in the black and white portrait of Alex. If it's a passport photo, the customs agent would think twice before letting this ferocious person into the country. Look at the portraits of Elizabeth, of Eric, of Judy, of Chuck himself! It's as if the range of colors and the new brushwork have added some new psychological dimension to his work. As the viewer stepped closer to each canvas, these enormous faces dissolved like chimeras. In an act of sublime legerdemain, the portrait transformed into a radiant byzantine mosaic. See how the canvas is a grid and each tile of the grid is bejeweled with a gaudy colorful circle or lozenge or rectangular shape. Close had found a whole new quirky vocabulary that had the joy of scat singing. The subject of the new paintings was no longer the human face examined in exquisite objectivity; the new subject was simply this: the sheer physical joy of the act of painting. In a flash, Chuck Close had become the most painterly painter in the country, producing the most exciting new painting I had seen in a long while. They were great paintings: great in their virtuosity, their daring, their confidence, their joy, their psychological insight. The new work in no way devalued the earlier work. It amplified it. The journey any artist travels had taken a major leap. But this was the detail of which I had to remind myself: These paintings were

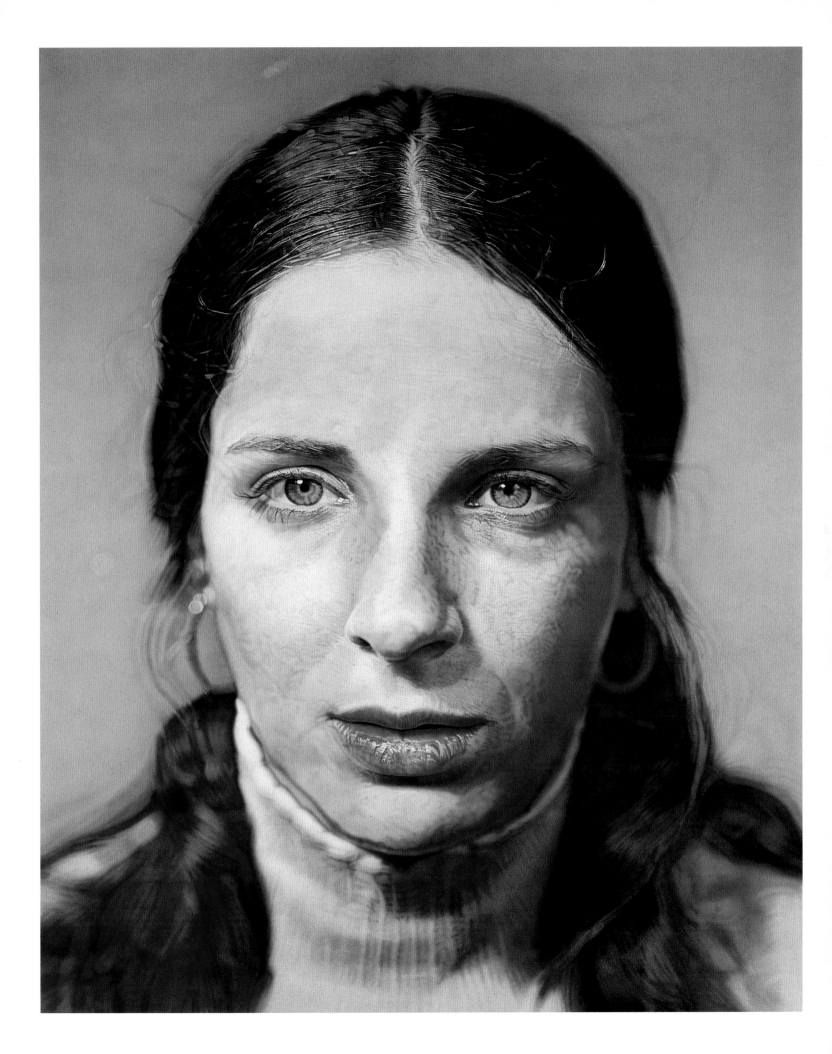

Installation of Chuck Close paintings
at The Pace Gallery, New York,
September-October 1988
Below: CINDY. Right: FRANCESCO I.

painted by a paralyzed man.

I have an acquaintance who is an expert on everything to do with art in all its manifestations. I regularly bump into him on my regular Saturday morning SoHo crawls, so it was no surprise to see him that day standing under Chuck's canvases. He said knowingly: "Lucky Chuck. Wouldn't you know? He has his catastrophe and becomes a great painter."

"But it's a great story!" I could imagine myself exclaiming to a movie executive who leans back from his Biedermeier desk as I pitch this surefire project. "Look at it!" I say. "A brilliant artist at the height of his powers is suddenly paralyzed, but he goes on to become an even greater painter. Upbeat. Inspirational. An American *My Left Foot*, *The Miracle Worker* about art, a bohemian *Regarding Henry*. A hip *Lust for Life*. Once again, tragedy and illness make you a better per-

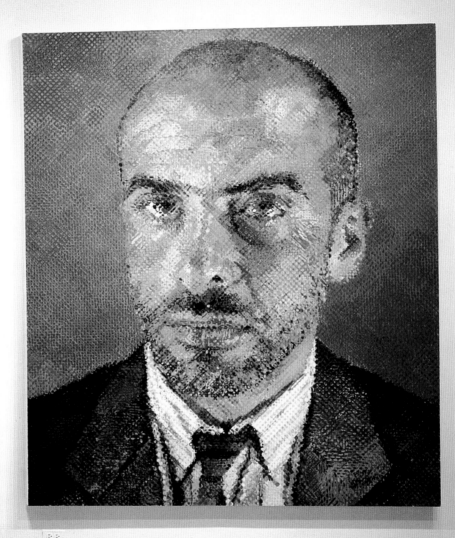

son and a better artist."

The exec wants to know Close's age. "We don't want any old artists. Hmm. Born in 1940? Jack Nicholson. He has a family? Wife and two daughters? Emma Thompson for the wife. Make the daughter the kid from *The Piano*. One daughter. Save a salary. He's got a doctor. Sharon Stone. Wait—" The exec is cooking. "Don't make the artist successful. Make him struggling and misunderstood until the catastrophe happens. What's the finale?"

The Metropolitan Museum of Art is giving Close a retrospective in 1997.

"Then your finale is the Retro at the Metro. Rocky with an easel instead of gloves. Does the Met have photogenic steps?"

The Met has photogenic steps.

"Do you know the guy? Can you get through to him?"

I had first met Chuck Close in the early eighties around New York at various parties where the worlds of art and theater and God knows what else collide. We did not, however, become friends until 1993, when my wife, Adele Chatfield-Taylor, who is president of the American Academy of Rome, persuaded Chuck, who is one of her trustees, and his wife, Leslie, who is a landscape historian, to come to Italy. Chuck had not traveled out of America since his—well, what do you call it? Catastrophe?

The exec asks: "He came to Italy. Did you talk about what happened in 1988? Share late-night secrets in the Coliseum? Was it all very ennobling?"

I hadn't noticed any ennobling. I had noticed a lot of fun. We traveled in a van. One day Chuck fell out of his wheelchair onto the gearshift, almost sending us into the Arno. But you know what? We roared with laughter! To go through the Giotto chapel with Chuck! To see the Renaissance through Chuck's eyes . . .

The exec frowns. "A lot of fun is no story. The audience needs inspiration. Where's the inspiration?"

I frown. Is that all the Close story is? Another inspirational anecdote about disease ennobling the victim? Where's the story?

"What happened between the time of—what else to call it?—the catastrophe and how he got back to work? Find out," says the imaginary executive. "There's your story."

So, in the fall of 1994, I asked Chuck Close what had happened in December 1988.

"This happened," he said, looking down at his Quickie wheelchair, his hands folded in his lap.

Chuck Close sits in his studio in Lower Manhattan. When I came in, he had extended his hand in greeting but his fingers cannot close in a grip. His legs are in braces. His manner is bright, objective, and his mood is cheery, even though he's dressed in the requisite downtown black. But then I am, too. The only color in the spare white studio in downtown Manhattan radiates from his latest canvas, a glowing portrait of the then-ninety-year-old painter Paul Cadmus. I step closer. The canvas dissolves into this celebration of paint.

"But how do you paint?"

Chuck shows me. I see that his upper arms can move. Thanks to Velcro, Chuck has the ability to strap a rather primitive hand brace to his right hand and arm. With both hands he then picks up his paintbrush and places it sideways between his teeth. He then leans over a slot built into the hand brace, clenches his teeth, pushes the brush firmly into place, sits up and is ready to paint.

I get right into what I hadn't asked him on our Italian trip. "Do you call what happened to you a catastrophe?"

"I don't think anyone would call their own event a catastrophe," says Chuck. "It's such a loaded term. But what do I call what happened to me? I call what happened to me an event. It's just something that happened."

"Your work seemingly changed direction after the event. How responsible is the event for the change in your work? What I'm trying to say is this: Are you in any way grateful to your event?"

Chuck smiles. "It is amazing. People actually do ask me that question. Was all this"—he says, pointing to the Cadmus painting—"worth all this?" he says, indicating his wheelchair. As if the event of 1988 is responsible for transforming me from one kind of an artist to another, as if my life as an artist changed all thanks to one day."

But his life as a human being *did* change—permanently—thanks to one day. So I ask him the question again. "What did happen on that day? Or is this too painful to talk about?"

Chuck shrugs. "Not at all. You know it happened on December 7, 1988, the forty-seventh anniversary of Pearl Harbor."

Chuck speaks with a matter-of-fact intensity, clarity, and even a buoyancy that belies what I am about to hear.

He woke up that morning with pains shooting through the center of his chest down both his arms and out into the tips of his fingers. It had to be angina. He tried to get out of bed but could barely stand. He leaned against the wall. He had been here before.

Years earlier a similar pain had woken him with such ugly intensity that surely it had to be something no less than death. Back then he had decided not to wake up Leslie and worry her. No, the simplest thing to do that night would be to sit up in bed stoically and wait for one of two things: either to die, or for the pain to pass. When he realized he wasn't going to die, he woke Leslie and told her. They went to doctors who would strap Chuck onto tables and do EKGs. One doctor gave him nitroglycerin to stick under his tongue, which he carried around for years but never used. Once when he was in Japan in 1986, working on a woodblock print, he became exhausted and had the pain again, but he laid it all down to jet lag and lack of sleep. He checked into a hospital in Kyoto where nobody spoke any English. The Japanese medics gave him more nitroglycerin for the flight home, but no one could ever find anything wrong with his always perfect heart. Was it stress? Hypertension? He had taken drugs for hypertension.

But now it was December 7, 1988, and the pain had returned. Only it wasn't the middle of the night. Leslie wasn't there. She had already gone off to her job at Wave Hill Center for Environmental Studies up in Riverdale, the Bronx. His two daughters, Georgia and Maggie, had gone off to school. He was alone in their apartment on the Upper West Side of Manhattan. He decided not to telephone for help. He would push up against the kitchen table, trusting the pain would stop as it had before. He would quiet himself by focusing in on all the things he had to do that day. There would be no painting that day. Today was a chore day. Talk on National Public Radio about the role of an artist in the current eighties art market. Buy Leslie a present for their wedding anniversary coming up on Christmas Eve. Give an award at Gracie Mansion, the mayor's residence, to an artist in the public school system before going over to the Pace Gallery Christmas party. Wasn't the Christmas season beginning earlier every year? They had a baby-sitter for the evening. He and Leslie would go out to dinner, get home early. The pain subsided. See. Nothing to it.

He needed fresh air. He walked diagonally across Central Park over to the East Side where all his chores were. Breathe deep. The weather report says forty-one degrees and fair. Beautiful. Yes, much better. These episodes of pain always occur when he's run down. His last show had closed only six weeks before. Even if he didn't admit it, a show always took a lot out of him. Stress and the role o

an artist. Try talking about that on Public Radio. He sees an antique pin in the window of a small jewelry store on Madison Avenue
that Leslie will like. He buys it and sticks it in his pocket. But he
wants to get Leslie something else. Dammit. He just doesn't feel
well.

Howard Read, director of photography at the Robert Miller
Gallery on East 57th Street, remembers Chuck coming in that day,
his usual robust normal self. Nothing out of the ordinary. Chuck
wanted to look at the flower photos of Robert Mapplethorpe that
Leslie loved. Howard made Polaroids of two of the flowers for him.
Chuck would choose later which one he'd buy. Today was not a
day to choose.

Chuck cut over to Second Avenue and down to 43rd Street to
the NPR studio to tape a segment of "All Things Considered." I
send away for the tape. Listening to that program years later,
Chuck's voice that December day sounds different, muffled and

fuzzy at first. Chuck answers that art used to belong to the part of the brain that thinks. Now it seems to have shifted over in the public's mind to the part of the brain that chooses what covering you'll put on the seat of your car. When did art move over to the world of style? Not his concern. Nor did he know about art as an investment. "It's antithetical to what I do. I don't want to think about art that way. Artists are not a critical part of the chic society." Chuck sees the big change in the 1988 art world in the new power of the collector. The hit list used by collectors who want the all-time favorites is now the same as the hit list used by museums. Collectors can pay that extra dollar and get the work they want, so a Van Gogh at auction can end up in the private room of a steak house in Japan.

Installation of Chuck Close paintings at The Pace Gallery, New York, November-December 1991
Left: ALEX. Above: JUDY.

Tina Barney. THE CLOSE FAMILY II (detail). 1992.
CHROMOGENIC COLOR PRINT, 48 X 60".
COURTESY JANET BORDEN, INC., NEW YORK

By the end of the tape his voice is strong and funny.

I can figure out the timetable of the day. It must be 4:00 now. Chuck is at East 43rd Street. In two hours he has to present an art award at Gracie Mansion, which is at 88th Street and East End Avenue. He decides to walk there. He loves to walk. He feels rotten. He's been coughing in violent spasms for the past few weeks. Chuck, who had no doctor, had stopped by a SoHo health clinic the week before and been given a dose of antibiotics. No, they hadn't worked. The coughing was still there. The cough must have turned into a cold. He stops at a Yorkville neighborhood bar to have a Scotch. He'll nip this cold in the bud and catch the five o'clock news till it's time to go. The big story on the news is of course the forty-seventh anniversary of Pearl Harbor. A member of Bush's economic team affirms the president's pledge not to raise taxes. The Irangate prosecution announces it will limit the evidence to be introduced against Oliver North. Time to go. Pay the bill. Does Chuck notice Doctor's Hospital as he passes it on his way into Gracie Mansion? A group called the Alliance for the Arts has invited ninety-five people to the mayor's house tonight for their annual awards ceremony. Waiters pass food through the crowd. Chuck hasn't eaten but he can't eat these lumpy things on trays. He feels queasy and wishes he hadn't had that Scotch. He's handed a schedule. The evening will be chaotic in spite of the mayor's office scheduling this awards ceremony down to the minute. The program is to begin at 6:10 when the mayor comes in. Mayor Ed Koch will then introduce the speakers. Chuck, who is the third speaker, will be introduced by Gerald Schoenfeld, chairman of the Shubert Organization, at 6:54. Chuck will read the citation at 6:55, and the winner, Louis Spanier, a teacher in Brooklyn, will accept his award at 6:58.

Chuck's chest hurts. It's hard to breathe. How can he get out of here?

Agnes Gund, a noted collector who is now the chairman of the board of The Museum of Modern Art, saw Chuck in the crowd that night and came over with the express purpose of asking him something she had been meaning to ask him for quite a while. Would he paint her portrait? If she had heard his interview about collectors a few hours before, she would have hesitated. Agnes Gund told me in 1994 how she remembered that event.

"He was sharp with me, even impatient. It was so unlike him. He told me he only painted friends, that he never took commissions. How he chooses who he paints. He was painting other painters. I understand that now. We've talked about it since. But that evening I took it personally."

Chuck and the various speakers were tapped to step up on the dais. Kitty Carlisle Hart, chairman of the New York State Council on the Arts, wanted to go first as she had an opening of something NYSCA supported, the Alvin Ailey Company. No. There could be no changes in the schedule. This was going to be one of those over-booked New York evenings. Chuck was seated between the poet John Ashbery and the president of the Board of Education, Robert Wagner, Jr., who had grown up in this house as the son of a former mayor. Chuck and Ashbery had met casually around town over the years. The two of them exchanged pleasantries. Years later, in light of what happened after, Ashbery remembered being struck by the fact that he saw nothing out of the ordinary about Chuck's state.

Mayor Koch came in on time at 6:10, talking to people along the way up to the dais, shaking hands, acknowledging applause. Ashbery wondered why Chuck suddenly got up and went over to speak with the woman running the event. Chuck was telling her how he felt. "I said this is no good. The pain was too great." She showed him the carefully planned schedule. Chuck would be finished in forty-five minutes and then he could leave. It was 6:15 now and Koch hadn't even begun speaking. "I said to the woman running the event I was sorry but I wasn't going to be able to go third. They had to let me give the award right after Koch's speech. Then I would have to go across the street to Doctor's Hospital." No, he did not need an ambulance. He returned to his seat.

Koch, being a showman/politician, enjoyed these events and began a long-winded speech obviously embellishing his prepared remarks: "Good evening and welcome to Gracie Mansion. The awards . . . presented tonight . . . ongoing effort . . . encourage interaction . . . New York City's public schools . . . matchless cultural resources . . . reach out to schoolchildren . . ."

Chuck is sitting on the dais holding on.

"I still can't figure out why the hell I had to stay there and give this award when I was in such pain, but it's typically me," Chuck said to me in 1994. "Denial runs in my family."

It must be 6:20 now. Koch goes on: "Priceless investment . . . future well-being of these youngsters . . . future strength of our city. Thank you all and God bless."

Koch sits down to applause. Schoenfeld is alerted to the new order and introduces Chuck who walks to the dais to read this citation:

> Louis Spanier, visual arts coordinator, community school district 32, is being honored for bringing an appreciation of the visual arts to students in the Bushwick area of Brooklyn. Through collaboration with Studio in a School Association, Arts Partners, and Learning through Arts/Guggenheim Museum, Mr. Spanier has encouraged his students to face the challenges posed by the community and to use the arts to productively contribute to their neighborhood.

Louis Spanier came to the dais and accepted the certificate from Chuck. John Ashbery was surprised to see Chuck not return to his seat but instead stagger off the dais into the audience and leave Gracie Mansion. Ten minutes later, Chuck, accompanied by a policeman, walked off the street into Doctor's Hospital.

"The emergency room was empty. I mean they were advertising for patients. They put me down on a table. The ferocity of the chest pains made them assume it was cardiac. They gave me intravenous Valium. They gave me more and more painkillers. They had no idea what the problem was."

Chuck never lost consciousness. He instructed them to call his wife. The hospital caught Leslie as she was leaving their West Side apartment to meet Chuck at Pace's Christmas party. She was in the hall locking the door when she heard the ringing. She opened the door. She answered the phone.

And that's the way lives shatter.

Years later, sitting in a West Side coffee bar, Leslie remembered that night: "On the way to the hospital in a cab, I wasn't really that worried. I thought, 'Chuck's under stress. He has to get this stress under control.'"

But when Leslie walked into the emergency room shortly after seven o'clock, she realized this was hardly a case of stress. But no one could tell her what was wrong. The emergency room doctor in charge looked at Leslie in a way that made her feel very uncomfortable. What is happening? No one knew. Then Chuck went into a long, violent convulsion. His hands and legs flailed about in seizure. The nurses and doctor held him down. Then he was still. His arms and legs stopped moving. He never lost consciousness.

At first the emergency room staff thought the convulsion was a reaction to the drugs and that the paralysis was temporary, simply hysterical paralysis. Chuck could breathe with great difficulty. If he had been by himself or out in the country or in Gracie Mansion, he would have suffocated to death. The nurses began to suction his lungs.

They were still testing him for cardiac problems.

Leslie doesn't remember calling anyone, but suddenly everyone was around her, friends appearing, offering help. She found an antique pin in Chuck's jacket pocket. She saw two Polaroids of Mapplethorpe flowers. The emergency room doctor came up to her and said, "Aren't you Leslie Rose?" How did the doctor in the emergency room in charge of saving Chuck's life know her maiden name? The doctor had taken her to her junior high school prom on her first date in East Meadow, Long Island, which is why he had been staring at her when she came in. How was she? She felt as if she had gone into a dreamlike state. She wanted Chuck out of here. This emergency room did not feel like a real hospital.

Leslie got Chuck transferred on Friday, December 10, three days later, to the intensive care unit at University Hospital, part of the NYU Medical Center on 34th Street, where he was looked after by the hospital's regular attending physicians. Chuck had only the top quarter of each lung working. He had to have his lungs suctioned through his nose every two hours around the clock. He could barely breathe. His diaphragm stopped working. He was severely paralyzed from the shoulders down. His bladder didn't work. He had a terrible numbness in his limbs. No diagnosticians or specialists saw him till the weekend was over, Monday, December 13. Those doctors put a catheter into his heart to look at the arteries. They inserted a catheter smaller than a hair into his spinal column.

Anselm Kiefer.
GERMANY'S SPIRITUAL HEROES
(DEUTSCHLANDS GEISTESHELDEN). 1973.
OIL AND CHARCOAL ON CANVAS,
121 X 268 1/2".
THE ELI BROAD FAMILY FOUNDATION

By now the doctors knew it was not cardiac and suspected it might be of neurological origins. Such traumas were being tested at University Hospital, but because Chuck had not been in an accident he didn't present the right symptoms that they could read. If Chuck had suffered the kind of visible, public injury a football player sustains on the playing field, the hospital would have known what to do. Even ambulances at this time were routinely administering steroids to accident victims. Why steroids? Because a shot of steroids administered immediately after an injury reduces the swelling in the affected area and produces a tremendous success rate in recovery. But Chuck's event was internal, private. No one could see anything. By the time the doctors gave Chuck the steroids to reduce possible swelling in his spinal column, days had passed.

"The steroids kept me awake—I mean awake—for twelve days. For twelve days until Christmas Eve, I hallucinated around the clock these wide-awake daymares. I thought we were in a constant earthquake. Everything was shaking, but I did not move. The world lost all color and became black and white. I had these visions that were very much like **Anselm Kiefer** paintings with their one-point perspective, that vanishing point right in the middle. I would usually be moving in these daymares, only I was never walking. I was always in my bed. No, not strapped down. There was no need to strap me down, because I couldn't move. I could move my head a bit. I could look down and see my feet at the bottom of the bed covered with a white sheet and feel the building shaking, the bed shaking, and feel the bed hovering above the floor. I moved through huge cavernous halls whose design reminded me of those by the Nazi architect Albert Speer. No sound. Simply flying like a jet through these spaces of Nazi Germany, rushing up to walls. I'm terrified I will crash into the wall, but then a door opens and I pass into another hall. I rush through that space until I'm flying through a night sky with clouds streaming by. I look behind me and see other people flying in their beds over this quaking universe. I'm the lead duck, leading them over this turbulent ocean until I see below me an aircraft carrier. My bed banks and dives, all the beds follow me, swooping down and landing on the deck of the aircraft carrier. I was not able to walk on the aircraft carrier. I stayed in the bed. Twelve days of that. The doctors said the episodes I experienced on these steroids are very much like a psychotic breakdown. When I was calmer, I realized Anselm Kiefer has his finger on the pulse of some kind of psychotic vision because to this day it is a very clear memory."

A host of doctors put Chuck through a series of tests best described as hideous and dangerous. "But when you go into a teaching hospital like NYU," Chuck remembers, "you have all these fledgling doctors each trying to figure out the right diagnosis for the express purpose of scoring points. Essentially, their efforts became this futile game of finding a needle in the haystack. Leaving no stone unturned, the medics even made Leslie go into my studio to check what hazardous materials I might have been using as an artist."

Could the very tools that made Chuck an artist have caused this unnameable horror? Does irony go that far, and is it that cruel? What a good scene this will be for the movie version! I see researchers dressed in astronaut suits breaking into his sealed-off studio with dogs sniffing out tubes of paint. Bruce Willis cries out: "I've got the villain! Cadmium orange!"

The doctors pored over Chuck's medical history. He and Leslie were asked to remember everything. Chuck was always falling down and hitting his head. But that's just clumsiness. Were there any other dysfunctions? "I'm dyslexic but I don't think that's related to what happened to me that day." When he was a kid he had great weakness in his arms and legs after any strenuous activity, but they could never track down why or give it a name. The weakness did not stop him from being active. When he was eleven, a serious kidney infection did confine him to bed for part of a year. "Perhaps that forced inactivity helped me to be an artist. But then so did being an only child. I don't think any of the above was responsible for this paralysis."

Chuck lay motionless in his bed in intensive care wondering how he would support his family. The steroid daymares were over. The realistic nightmares had begun.

"My first thought was since I'm going to be paralyzed, I'll have to become a conceptual artist. I'll think the art out, and someone else will execute it for me. That was a very discouraging prospect, because I have always enjoyed the physicality of painting. But I thought maybe it would be like those collaborations where you made woodcuts with the Japanese masters who carry out your work with their skills."

But as the days went by, he was far more peaceful than he had any reason to be, even if it was the peace of a car wreck. "Have you ever been in a car wreck with the car spinning out of control? You know that strange eerie calmness that takes over as you almost go into slow motion? You turn the wheel this way, that way. Only when it's all over do you fall apart and go into shock. This was an attenuated, drawn-out case of that, where many many days I experienced a profound calmness, eerie even to me."

Part of that calm came from Leslie's constant presence. Leslie wanted Chuck to see that his world was still intact, that she was there, that the girls were there. But she looked at Chuck, and, from her point of view, her world was no longer intact.

Chuck was totally aware of what was going on. "I would look at the panic in Leslie's eyes, and I felt so sorry for what I was putting her through."

Chuck felt calm and strangely positive as he let Leslie know his main fear: "That I was not going to make art. Since I'll never be able to move again, I would not be able to make art. I watched my muscles waste. These hollows in my hands—what do they call it? The fleshy Mound of Venus here between the thumb and index finger was becoming indented. My hands didn't work. I needed to get my hands to work. I was very strong before. I did a lot of work in the garden at our house in the country. I walked. I was very active. I weighed 210 and stood six-three. I had the body of a much younger man as well as the bald head of an older man. Being bald when you are twenty, you're used to never looking the way you want to look, but I thought I had a decent body. I took pleasure in my body."

One day Chuck realized that he had just enough head movement so that if a brush was placed between his teeth, he could control it enough to paint. "I suddenly became encouraged. I tried to imagine what kind of teeny paintings I could make with only that much movement. I tried to imagine what those paintings might look like. Hospital imagery? It didn't matter. Even that little bit of neck movement was enough to let me know that perhaps I was not powerless. Perhaps I could do something myself."

They still didn't know what had happened to Chuck.

And then they did.

Dr. Kristjan T. Ragnarsson, Chuck's physiatrist (a doctor who treats persons

33

with physical disabilities) described to me in 1994 what had happened to Chuck in 1988. It has a name as does everything. Even *Untitled* can be a name for a painting. Anterior Spinal Artery syndrome is the name of what happened to Chuck's spinal cord during that violent convulsion in the emergency room.

I write down the technical part to make sure it's accurate.

"The cervical spine, which is also referred to as the neck, contains seven bones and eight cervical nerve roots that come from the spinal cord inside the spine and go to the neck, shoulders, and arms. The cervical nerve roots are numbered C-1 starting just below the head at the top of the neck running down through C-8 located just above the first rib. When his paralysis struck, it was caused by damage to the spinal cord from a blood clot at the level of C-3, the third cervical nerve root, high up in the neck. If the clot had struck at C-8, the lowest cervical nerve root, Chuck would have suffered minimal paralysis in his upper limbs. If the clot had struck at either C-1 or C-2, it would have killed him instantly. If Chuck had been alone when he was struck by the clot's assault on C-3, he could have very quickly suffocated to death."

I ask the doctor how it struck.

"Like any other organ of the body, the spinal cord has its own blood flow. The main blood vessel to the spinal cord is called the anterior spinal artery. For some reason, on December 7, 1988, a blood clot lodged within this artery in the neck, disrupting the blood flow, and damaging the spinal cord, almost as if it had suffered a traumatic injury. It is certainly possible that the disrupted blood flow was caused by the same factors that had given him weakness in his arms and legs since childhood, but it is impossible to prove that. There was no evidence of aneurysm. No, only a blood clot."

How would the doctor describe his patient in medical terms?

"Chuck Close is a person with incomplete tetraplegia—also known as quadriparesis or incomplete quadriplegia."

Incomplete?

"If Chuck had complete quadriplegia, none of his limbs would have any movement and he could not feel his hands or legs at all. But his upper arms move, and he has feeling and some movement in his legs. Therefore, incomplete."

Now they knew what he had; but, for what he had, there is no cure.

It was now the end of January 1989.

Leslie knew Chuck was miserable and would have to find a way to get back to work as quickly as possible. Chuck would have to be moved into a rehabilitation center to exercise, to work, to learn how to get back to the business of life. Surely Chuck could walk again. Yes? Perhaps? You have to hope. Leslie and their friend, the painter Mark Greenwold, went to investigate the Rusk Institute, which is another part of the NYU medical complex. They burst into tears when they saw the broken bodies, the stroke victims, the patients tied to wheelchairs to prevent falling out. They wept when they saw Rusk's primitive equipment, all leather thongs and canvas straps and patients waiting in line to use these archaic pulleys. Where was the high-tech machinery? This was 1989. There must be glorious miracle-producing machines that would guarantee Chuck's return of powers. Leslie and their friend Barbara Harshman checked out rehabilitation centers near the city, out of the city. But they chose Rusk. It was in town, it had a great reputation, plus a therapeutic pool that could only do good, and most importantly, Chuck would have a private room. His friends, his children could visit him easily during visiting hours after 4:00 P.M. Leslie and the girls and his myriad of friends had all the high hopes in the world. Miracles happen. Right?

The primary agents of Chuck's miracle would be Phyllis Palsgrove, the occupational therapist, and Meg Sowarby, the physical therapist.

When Chuck came into Rusk, he could not even sit up straight in his wheelchair without being strapped into it. Were they disheartened by Chuck? That's not their business. What Meg and Phyllis saw was someone who desperately wanted to get better. They saw that Chuck would not be a patient as much as a collaborator.

Chuck's therapy sessions were from 8:00 A.M. to 4:00 P.M. Monday to Friday. His room, number 408, looks like a small cabin in tourist class on a 1950s ocean liner facing out onto the East River. The morning light streams in; traffic on the FDR highway hums by constantly, the *Daily News* plant is across the river in Queens, grinding out the news of the world. The room contained a small refrigerator. Chuck kept it fully stocked for the friends who flocked in every day. There was no sorrow in room 408. Nurses streamed in constantly asking them to keep the party noise down.

Rusk frowns on its patients using alcohol, but Chuck decided that if an occasional drink helped him, then he'd have the drink. "I said I'm getting through this any way I can, and I made it into a party."

How did Leslie feel about that? The fact is it didn't make any difference how Leslie felt. The truth is, as Leslie would quickly learn, at a rehabilitation center the family is in the way. The family has illusions and expectations that are unrealistic, and those unrealistic hopes only produce despair and anger in the patient and the family and make life generally difficult for the staff. The truth is miracles don't happen at a rehab. All the patient can do is protect what nature has restored. All the patient can do is figure out a way to get back to life in the rooms Rusk offers.

Meg and Phyllis showed me the exercise therapy room. Grim. But they point out that the Rusk patient doesn't need high-tech machinery. The Rusk patient needs simple canvas and leather devices on simple machines with simple weights and pulleys to strengthen whatever powers the patient has recovered. Chuck's hands still didn't work. His legs didn't move. And this is what Chuck was learning. You get back the lion's share of what you're going to get back in the first three months after your catastrophe. You get virtually everything you're going to get back in the first six months. You get minuscule amounts back in the next two years. It's virtually unheard of to get any return back after that.

This exercise room contained a tilt table onto which Chuck was strapped for a few minutes each day. Meg slowly moved it higher until, one day, for the first time in weeks, Chuck, strapped in, finally assumed a simple standing position that allowed his blood to flow through his organs. At Rusk an event like that is a triumph. Everyone applauded.

Meg and Phyllis showed me the four-foot-deep pool that contains six underwater seats and walk bars extending across the pool. Chuck had to confront the terror of executing the following herculean action: crossing the pool supported by water. Suppose he fell forward. He felt he would surely drown. Meg kept him up. She promised if he got better she'd take him out drinking.

Leslie's only power over his salvation was her insistence that Chuck get back to his occupation as a painter. Meg and Phyllis showed me the occupational therapy room. It looks like a kindergarten classroom with its low toddler tables. But at a rehabilitation center you learn that occupational therapy is not designed to get you back to your occupation. Occupational therapy is the room where athletes and students and dancers and CEOs of large corporations and housewives and *people* learn to stack large yellow spools on top of each other; it's the room where they learn how to put their laundry into the washing machine, the room where they learn how to cook on the stove and take food out of the refrigerator and turn the water faucets on and off. This is the room designed to get the patient back to forming a new relationship with the simplest details of daily living.

And every patient's puzzle is how to solve that in his or her own personal way. Chuck had a puzzle-solving nature that Leslie understood and Phyllis fell into. Chuck had recovered movement in his upper arm. In this room, Leslie and Phyllis devised a hand splint onto which they could tape a paintbrush. They clamped a piece of shirt cardboard to a vise that they stuck to a kindergarten table. Phyllis brought Chuck crummy poster paint out of the chest of supplies, the gloppy kind kids use. With great effort, Chuck drew a primitive grid on this cardboard. He could barely move the upper portion of his arms. He moved the brush around in the paint for as long as he could bear it, that is, a second or two. He attempted to daub the splotch of poster paint onto the space of the penciled grid.

"The first thing I said to my wife and to Phyllis was 'I can't do it.' I remember that Leslie burst into tears. But actually what I did was very fraudulent. The truth was simpler and more devious. I had only told them I couldn't do it because I wanted them to say to me 'Yes, you can.' I wanted to get their encouragement. I wanted them to reassure me that this was in fact the first step and I shouldn't be disappointed. So at the same time I said 'I can't do it,' I was also thinking, 'Hey, I did put the paint onto the paper. This isn't so bad.' But I kept it my secret. I didn't let anybody know."

But they must have taken some encouragement. The next day Phyllis found space in something called the art therapy room. Chuck said, "Go see it. I'm not exaggerating. It was one of the most depressing places I've ever been to in my life." The room is not there anymore. The Institute has taken the space for a new entrance. But I can see what Chuck looked out onto: glass sliding doors off an abandoned plaza into which trash from the FDR blows. The view has the feel of a crummy motel outside Atlantic City where losers sleep off their failure. For an artist in 1989, this room must have held a particular horror. Art? Terrible crude drawings dangled from clotheslines. Half-finished baskets were left abandoned on tables. Whoever considered burning designs onto a piece of wood artistic? Chuck said, "It's hard enough to make art when you devote your life to it. It's agony to see grown men and women struggling over paintings a five-year-old would throw away." Phyllis made Chuck a wheelchair-accessible easel that could hold a 24-by-30-inch canvas. His legs could be slid underneath it. Leslie asked a longtime studio assistant named Michael Volonakis to help her transport what was necessary to make a painting from Chuck's studio on Spring Street up to Rusk. Chuck could barely hold up his arm. "I painted with the brush held in both hands. I had to have Michael or Leslie pull the brush out of the storage rack and shove it into the brush holder strapped to my hand. I would ask them to give me the green brush—no, not that one—the yellow-green brush. I began regaining movement as well as strength. I could make a lozenge shape and then my hands would drop back in my lap. I saw that each grid was in fact a tiny painting. I thought about making little teeny paintings. I'll paint in my lap little two-inch paintings backed with Velcro and then they'll all go together on the wall like a big jigsaw puzzle. It will eventually build into a big picture. I didn't want to lose the scale of my work. This would address the problem of how I'd build a big painting. I'd paint little pictures and then have assistants mount them on the wall."

I look at the Paul Cadmus on the studio wall, its series of grids, each containing these primitive shapes. Each square is its own painting.

"But isn't that what you've done?" I ask.

"That's exactly what I did. Only I did it all on one surface."

I ask him about the pictorial vocabulary he developed in the hospital. How did he learn to trust that the simplest of shapes, the diamond, the lozenge, the square, could carry out the weight of his intentions. Does that go back to his time at Yale? Josef Albers was no longer there, but his influence must still have been in the air. Also the shapes have a cartoon quality that makes me think of the last great period of Philip Guston, who taught Chuck at Yale in the sixties.

Philip Guston.
PAINTING, SMOKING, EATING. 1973.
OIL ON CANVAS, 77 1/2 X 103 1/2".
COLLECTION THE STEDELIJK MUSEUM, AMSTERDAM

Chuck Close.
DRAWING FOR
PHIL/RUBBER STAMP
(detail).1976.
INK ON PAPER,
7 5/8 X 6 1/2".
Private collection. New York

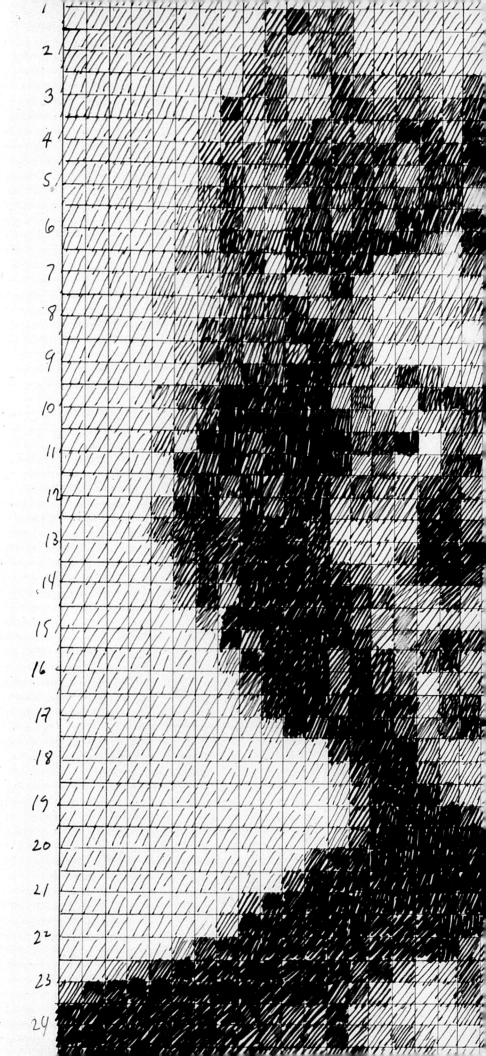

Chuck considers a scant millisecond before responding: "I think my reliance on those shapes came out of the mix of ideas which were in the air in the late sixties when the dominant mode was one of severe reductiveness. Because my state, my quadriplegia as incomplete as it was, pared everything down for me to its essence. I was as pared down to the essence as anyone could be and still be alive. One of the things the sixties was about was a belief in the process, a belief that the process would set you free. All you had to do was follow the process wherever it would take you. In the sixties, artists were looking for materials that didn't have any kind of built-in historical baggage. Materials like bronze were so heavily laden with history that it was hard to use them without making the results look like every other piece of bronze. So artists went to Canal Street and they bought rubber or lead or other unartistic materials and took them home to see what they could do with them and still have it be art. Well, you could lean the rubber against the wall or coil it or pile it or shred it or eat it. Just let the rubber or whatever simply be. Richard Serra and Robert Smithson, my contemporaries, all of us coming

Chuck Close. PHIL (detail).
1969.
SYNTHETIC POLYMER ON CANVAS, 108 X 84".
Collection the Whitney Museum
of American Art, New York.
Purchase, with funds from
Mrs. Robert M. Benjamin. 69.102

up together at the same time, had a belief that if you only have the courage to back yourself into your own corner you would find your way out, but if you stay in the middle of the room you'll be with everyone else and only everybody else's solution will occur to you. We believed that problem creating was more interesting than or at least as interesting as problem solving, that if you can ask yourself the interesting question, the solution will come, that you must purge yourself of the ghosts of everyone else's solutions by putting yourself in the position where none of their answers is applicable. Willem de Kooning's solution or Frank Stella's solution fit for them but wouldn't fit for you. But if you follow the process wherever it goes, if you listen for a different drumbeat, odds are you will find your own answer. Philip Glass was doing that in music, The Living Theater in performance art. The artist had to get into trouble because if you could get yourself into trouble, you had a wonderfully naive belief that a new answer would come. So this is all I knew. I was an artist. I was in trouble. Nobody had any answers that would apply to me. I had to accept where I was and see where it took me. In that horrible room, I painted every day."

What was the first painting you finished?

"Alex II, the portrait of Alex Katz. Leslie saw it. She cried. But with pleasure. Although the image of Alex was profoundly sad and angry, the painting itself had a more colorful palette than my work had had previously. Alex's face may have shown rage, but the colors I used seemed optimistic, even cheerful. I felt things were going to be all right."

I ask Chuck if this was the first time a psychological statement entered into a Close work. Was this piece a breakthrough?

Chuck asks me to take down a catalog from a shelf. "Look at the last painting I did before my, whatever you want to call it. Look at the painting of

Francesco Clemente

. The surface is already beginning to dissolve. But it captures the aesthetic beauty of Clemente's face. Look at the Cindy Sherman portrait I painted before the event. This was the path I had been on, this dissolution of the image. I realized in that horrible room at Rusk that all I had done was catch up in my work with where I had been. I'm not in the business of reinventing the wheel. I'm dyslexic. I have to stay on the track."

But what was the biggest change in your work?

Chuck Close.
FRANCESCO I (detail). 1987-88.
OIL ON CANVAS, 100 X 84".
Collection Ron and Ann Pizzuti, Columbus, Ohio

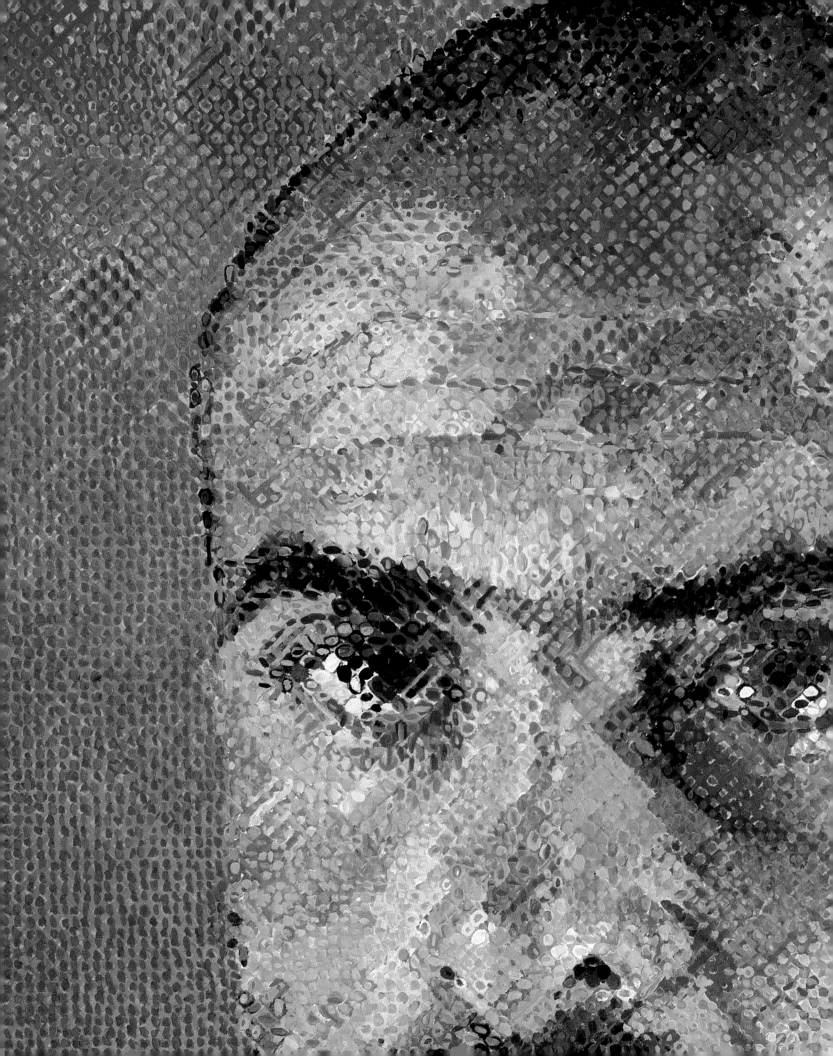

"The big change—in addition to everything else physically—was the palette I used. When I was a kid and starting as an abstract expressionist before I found my own vision, my main influence had been de Kooning. I admired the way **de Koon-ing** incorporated the human figure into abstract expressionism. He's always showing you how a particular painting happened. There's lots of generosity on that canvas. There is no mystery involved in his work. He had a very personal palette. I used a lot of de Kooning color in my early work. When I finally met de Kooning in the early eighties, I said it was a pleasure to meet someone who had painted a few more de Koonings than I had."

I'd love to see those early paintings.

"No," says Chuck as buoyantly as he says everything else. "I don't have those early paintings. Destroyed them all. I kept one, which I lent to my college for an art show, and a fire destroyed it."

Is Chuck a Zen master? No, he's too matter-of-fact and cheery for that. He's just practical. I think he might be the most realistic and accepting person I've ever met.

"When I gave up abstract expressionism and started painting my large pictures, I also gave up using de Kooning's palette. As someone influenced by minimalism, I only used the three primary colors. I loved de Kooning but had to leave his influence to get on with my own work. I needed to build my own colors out of a very simple palette of red, yellow, blue. But in this hospital, in that grim gray dank room, I went back to making the colors I used when I was under the influence of de Kooning. That was my life at Rusk. I did my therapy and had my daily visits from my friends and painted and painted and painted. My physical therapist, Meg, made good on her promise. She'd pack me into a wheelchair and load me into a van and we'd go out and get drunk as skunks. She'd get me back to the hospital by midnight before my wheelchair turned into a pumpkin. One wonderful night six patients and six therapists went to an incredibly crowded disco. Hundreds of sweating, surging bodies all around and there in the middle of the floor were six patients in six wheelchairs like covered wagons in a circle dancing from the waist up, joyously screaming our lungs out, waving our arms, whatever we could move!"

When did you know you would leave Rusk?

"I had a month's notice that I'd be released in August 1989, seven months after getting there. The doctors wanted me to stay longer, but the therapists and I could see that the effects of physical therapy were tapering off.

Also Chuck wanted to go home. Weekend visits home were not allowed by the insurance company, which does not like paying for an empty bed.

"We had a truck. Leslie and Michael came, and we packed up my gear from Rusk and drove out to our country house. I swore I would continue to see the other patients at Rusk, but it's like a friendship on a cruise ship . . . I left. It was the end of summer. When I got to the country, my kids had painted a big banner on the studio welcoming

FRANCESCO I (detail).

Willem de Kooning. WOMAN I. 1950-52.

OIL ON CANVAS, 6' 3 7/8 X 58".

THE MUSEUM OF MODERN ART, NEW YORK. PURCHASE.

Photograph © 1995 The Museum of Modern Art, New York

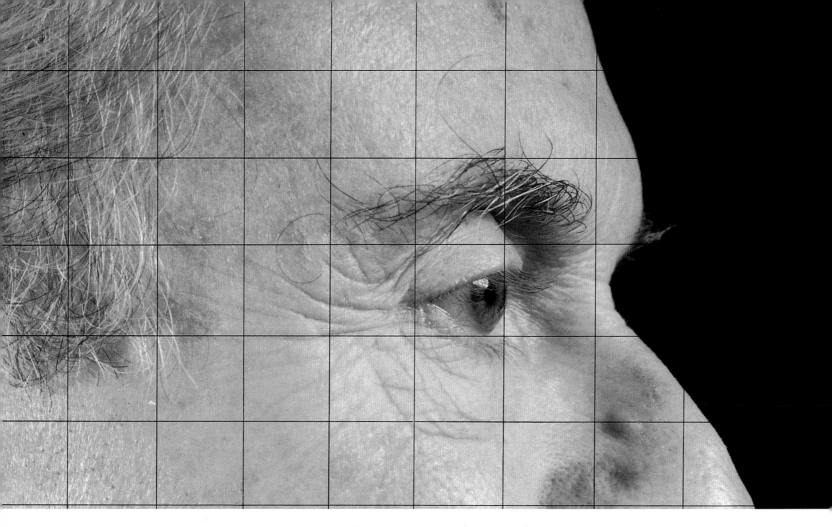

Chuck Close. Maquette for ROY (detail). 1993.
POLAROID PHOTOGRAPH, 20 x 24".
Courtesy Pace/MacGill Gallery, New York

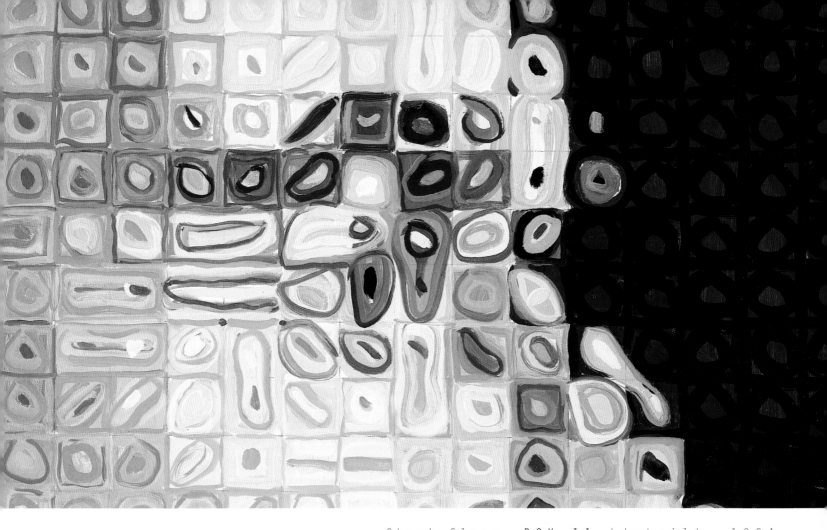

me back. There was a pool! Leslie had done battle with the town zoning board in order to get permission to install a swimming pool for me to continue my therapy. She had the bathrooms redesigned to be wheel-chair accessible. She installed what she hoped would be temporary ramps, but I feared they were permanent."

I ask him if he has periods of terrible anger.

Chuck shrugs. "Leslie would say I'm in denial. I don't feel I am."

"You have to have rage," I tell him. "In the inspirational movie of your life, your rage will be a big scene."

Chuck moves a switch on a box attached to his wheelchair. The motorized wheelchair glides him over to a table. He lifts a glass of water with his wrists and sips from it.

"When I saw that gimp movie *Born on the Fourth of July* and Tom Cruise started angrily banging up his room, I thought that's not my style because behavior like that doesn't get you what you want. If you're not a cooperator, you're shit out of luck. I want everybody to like me and think I'm a nice guy. This is very important for me and my persona, sometimes at the expense of what I want. *I* try to be what other people want me to be. If doctors want me to be a good patient, I'll be a good patient. If nurses and aides want me to co-operate, I'll cooperate. You can be at their mercy if they don't like you. If they don't want to clean you up after some bowel accident, you can lay there an awfully long time. My particular personality happened to dovetail quite nicely with the way to behave in a hospital."

But didn't Chuck undergo any spiritual illumination in the hospital? Didn't his condition take him to any higher place?

Chuck shrugged. "The first thing that occurred to me after those hallucinations passed was, gee, maybe I ought to pray. The atheist in the foxhole routine. If I was going to die in that hospital, and that was still a distinct possibility, I thought maybe praying might be the smart thing to do. I even became jealous in the weeks after of people around me who seemed to be able to draw on some kind of sustaining personal faith. I saw that faith wasn't strange or stupid but rather something that seemed to bring them peace. Except I had to remind myself that I'm not even an agnostic. I'm your basic garden variety atheist. But why not cover my bets? Isn't that Pascal's wager? Shouldn't I behave as if there might be a God? But then I asked what kind of God would inflict this event on me? And then, why would any self-respecting God even respond to an atheist's last-minute plea? I wouldn't have any respect for a God who would listen to prayers like mine. So

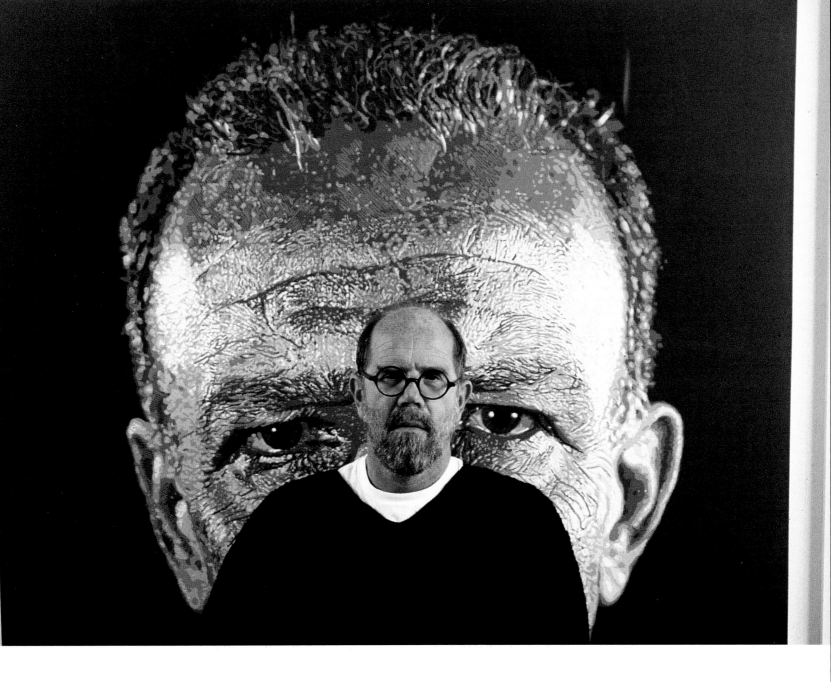

CHUCK CLOSE. 1994.

Photograph (detail) © Martha Cooper

I decided there was no reason to resort to prayer."

"You're telling me there is nothing inspirational about all this?" I ask him. "No rebellion. No fury. You were simply saved by the sixties and de Kooning and your identity as an artist and Leslie getting you back to that identity and Meg and Phyllis figuring out the way?"

"Perhaps. Nothing saved me. Everything saved me. It's all the luck of the draw. The heroes in all this are Leslie and my children. You see, I knew from the beginning that somehow I was going to get through this. Leslie and my daughters looked at me and saw this broken mess. It's been far more upsetting and depressing finally to the people around me than it's been to me."

I asked Leslie what the hard part is.

"The spontaneity is gone," she says. "We just can't go out at eleven P.M. the way we used to and take a long walk and pop into a Chinese restaurant, or when you're in the country and suddenly you go out into the woods and explore. Everything must be prepared. Nothing will ever change. And the assistants—who are wonderful—are always there. I feel sometimes that Chuck and I are never alone. But then you balance everything. Chuck is alive."

I go back to my imaginary movie producer. Forget it, I tell him. There's no story. No inspirational tack. No miracle. It's only the story of an artist who was saved by his identity as an artist.

"Hey," says the exec, "he's a disabled artist."

But no, Chuck Close is not that. He is an artist who was deflected momentarily from his path. He got back on it. He's an artist who happens to have a disability.

I return to Chuck's studio. Two new canvases of Roy Lichtenstein midway to completion hang on their easels. "If you never step back to get distance, how do you know that small grid of red and that small grid of pink is going to add up to the illusion of a shadow beside the eye?"

"It's the way a musician doesn't have to have the orchestra present to hear the sound of what he has written. The composer writes out the parts. I know how the colors will land."

"What do you call us? The ones who can walk?"

"Oh," Chuck brightens. He sits up in his wheelchair. "We call you the temporarily abled."

CHUCK CLOSE. 1994.
Photograph (detail) © Martha Cooper

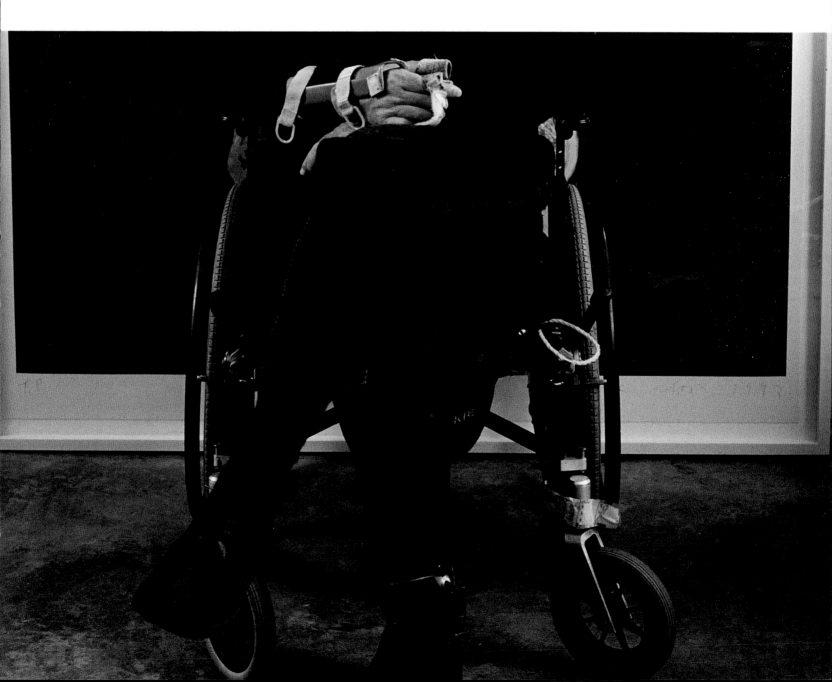

1 9 8 6 - 1 9 8 8

PLATES

1. SELF-PORTRAIT. 1986.
OIL ON CANVAS, 54 1/2 X 42 1/4".

2. ALEX. 1987.
OIL ON CANVAS, 100 X 84".

3. LUCAS I. 1986-87.
OIL ON CANVAS, 100 X 84".

4. LUCAS II. 1987.
OIL ON CANVAS, 36 X 30".

5. SELF-PORTRAIT. 1987.

OIL ON CANVAS, 72 X 60".

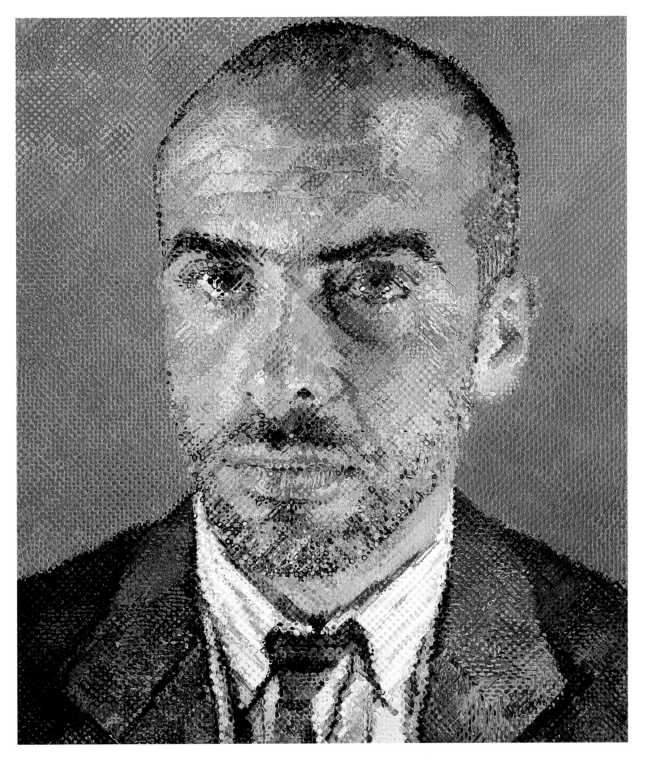

6. FRANCESCO I. 1987-88.
OIL ON CANVAS, 100 X 84".

7. CINDY. 1988.
OIL ON CANVAS, 102 X 84".

8. CINDY II. 1988.
OIL ON CANVAS, 72 X 60".

9. FRANCESCO II. 1988.
OIL ON CANVAS, 72 X 60".

1 9 8 8 - 1 9 9 5

ALEX II (detail).

10. ALEX II. 1989.
OIL ON CANVAS, 36 X 30".

Chuck Close at work on ELIZABETH.

11. ELIZABETH. 1989.
OIL ON CANVAS, 72 X 60".

66

JANET (detail).

12. JANET. 1989.
OIL ON CANVAS, 36 X 30".

JUDY (detail).

13. JUDY. 1990.
OIL ON CANVAS, 72 X 60".

ALEX (detail).

14. ALEX. 1990.
OIL ON CANVAS, 36 X 30".

MAQUETTE FOR BILL. 1990.
POLAROID PHOTOGRAPH, 20 X 24".

15. BILL. 1990.

OIL ON CANVAS, 72 X 60".

ERIC (in progress).

16. ERIC. 1990.
OIL ON CANVAS. 100 X 84".

APRIL (detail).

17. APRIL. 1990-91.
OIL ON CANVAS, 100 X 84".

MAQUETTE FOR ALEX. 1987.

POLAROID PHOTOGRAPH mounted on foamcore, 20 X 24". 1991.16.

Collection Lannan Foundation, Los Angeles

18. ALEX. 1991.

OIL ON CANVAS, 100 X 84".

BILL II (detail).

19. BILL II. 1991.
OIL ON CANVAS, 36 X 30".

"Lucas"

82

MAQUETTE FOR LUCAS. 1990.

POLAROID PHOTOGRAPH. 20 X 24"

20. LUCAS. 1991.

OIL ON CANVAS, 28 X 24".

Chuck Close at work on SELF-PORTRAIT.

21. SELF-PORTRAIT. 1991.

OIL ON CANVAS, 100 X 84".

MAQUETTE FOR JANET. 1987.

POLAROID PHOTOGRAPH, 20 X 24".

22. J A N E T.   1 9 9 2.
OIL ON CANVAS, 100 X 84".

JOHN (detail).

23. JOHN. 1992.

OIL ON CANVAS, 100 X 84".

MAQUETTE FOR RICHARD. 1991.
POLAROID PHOTOGRAPH. 20 X 24".

24. RICHARD (ARTSCHWAGER). 1992.
OIL ON CANVAS, 72 X 60".

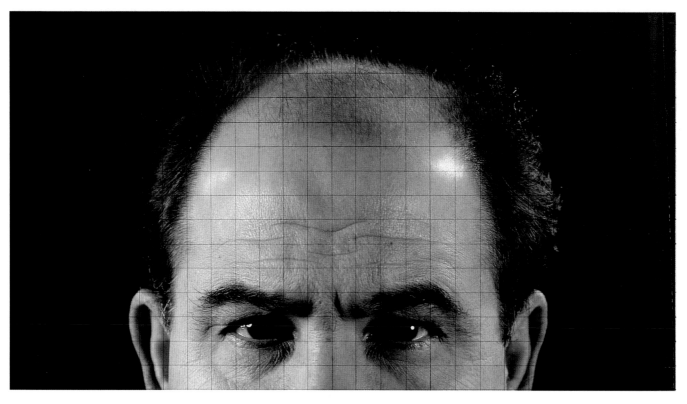

MAQUETTE FOR JOEL (detail). 1991.
POLAROID PHOTOGRAPH, 20 X 24".

25. JOEL. 1993.
OIL ON CANVAS, 102 X 84".

MAQUETTE FOR JOHN. 1992.

POLAROID PHOTOGRAPH, 20 X 24".

26. JOHN II. 1993.
OIL ON CANVAS, 72 X 60".

MAQUETTE FOR KIKI. 1992.

POLAROID PHOTOGRAPH, 20 X 24".

27. KIKI. 1993.
OIL ON CANVAS, 100 X 84".

MAQUETTE FOR SELF-PORTRAIT (detail). 1993.
POLAROID PHOTOGRAPH, 20 X 24".

28. SELF-PORTRAIT. 1993.
OIL ON CANVAS, 72 X 60".

PAUL (detail).

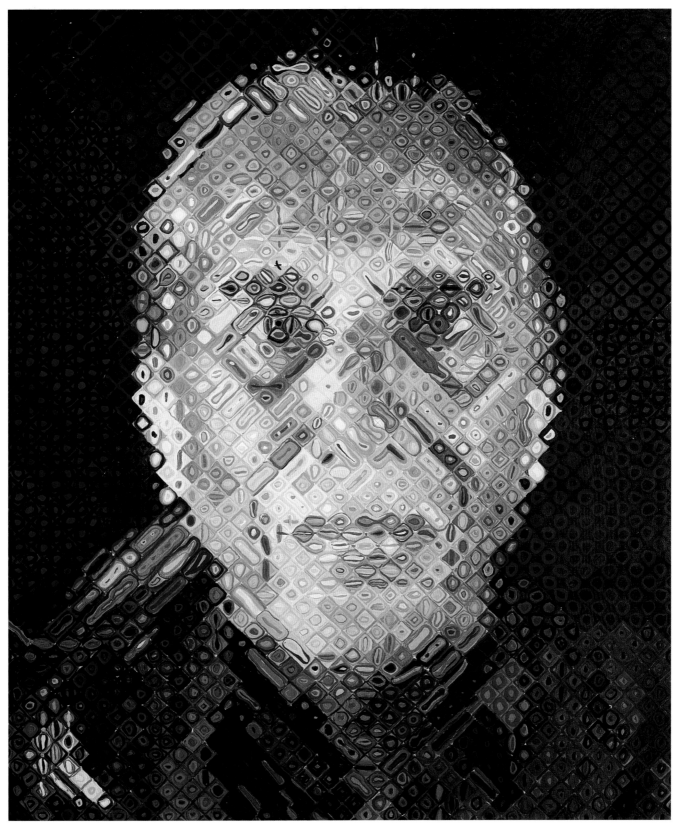

29. PAUL. 1994.
OIL ON CANVAS, 102 X 84".

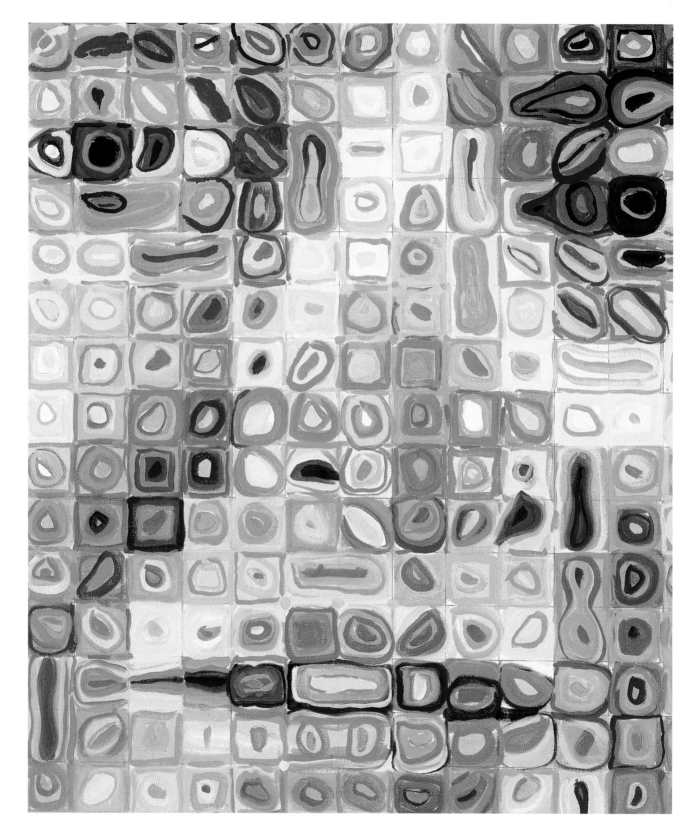

ROY I (detail).

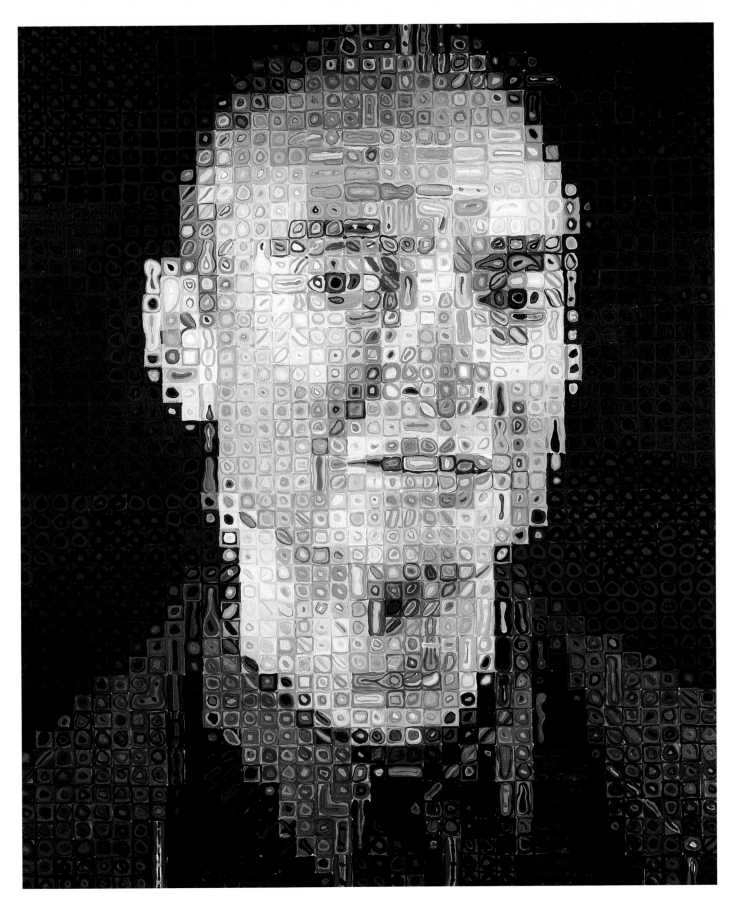

30. ROY I. 1994.
OIL ON CANVAS, 102 X 84".

"Roy II"

MAQUETTE FOR ROY. 1993.
POLAROID PHOTOGRAPH. 20 X 24".

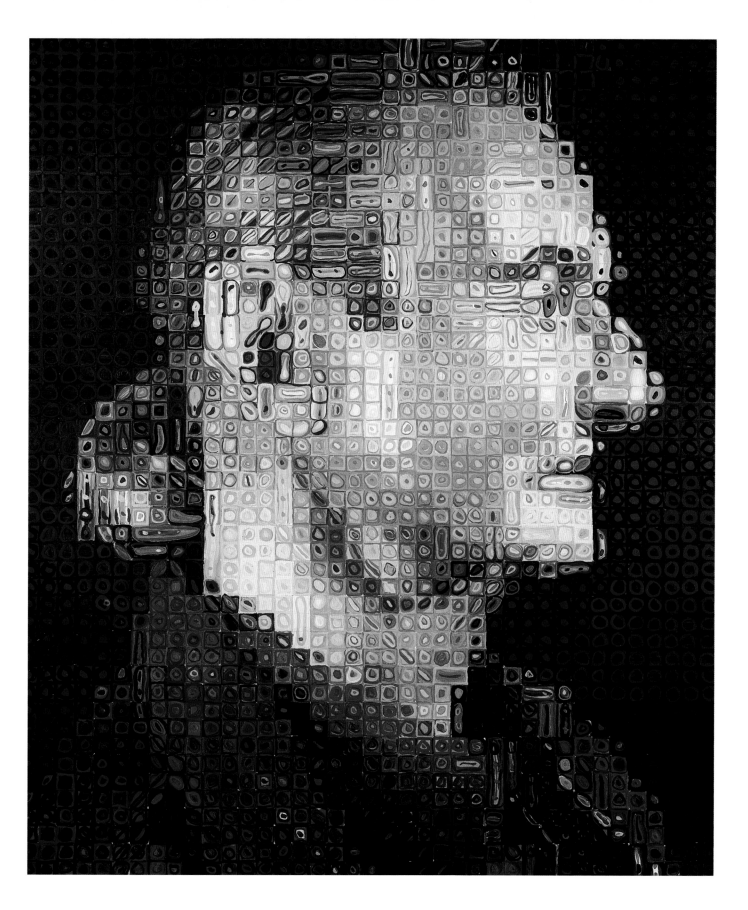

31. ROY II. 1994.
OIL ON CANVAS, 102 X 84".

MAQUETTE FOR DOROTHEA. 1995.

POLAROID PHOTOGRAPH. 20 X 24".

32. DOROTHEA. 1995.
OIL ON CANVAS, 102 X 84".

P O R T R A I T   O F   T H E

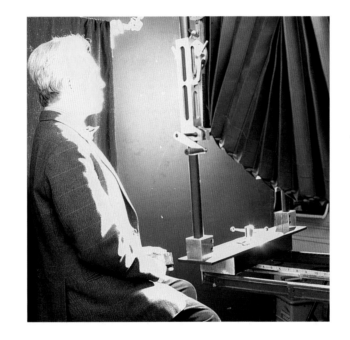

PLAYWRIGHT

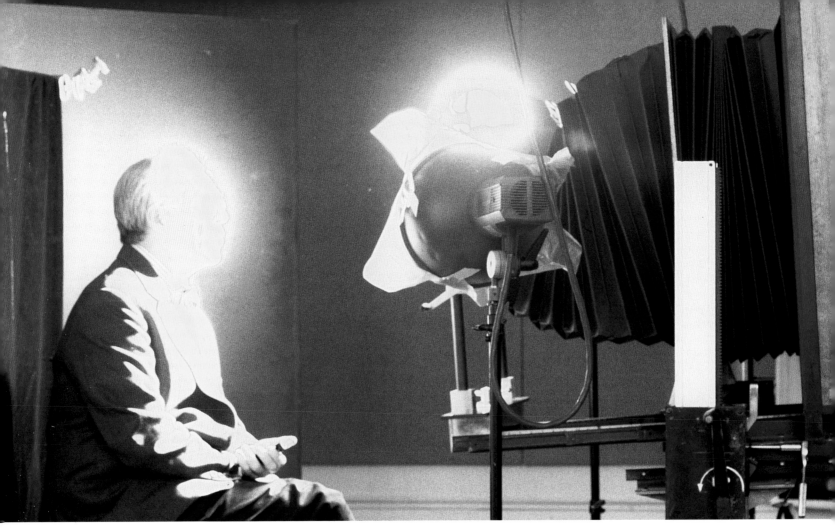

(Editor's Notes)

On December 13, 1994, John Guare sat for Chuck Close just as Chuck Close sat earlier in the year for his portrait by John Guare. Only this time the means of transcription was a series of 20 x 24" Polaroids taken by the artist. The Polaroid portraits Chuck Close takes of himself, family, and friends comprise an extraordinary bank of images Chuck refers to when looking for new subject matter and become integral to the process of his colossal paintings. Rarely exhibited or reproduced, these Polaroid "maquettes"--in themselves unique and compelling works of art--map out a human floor plan for Close's superhuman heads.

On the day of the photo session with John Guare, Chuck Close greets his visitors and his subject wearing a black Mao jacket, black slacks, and black shoes. In this setting, he is clearly the authority figure, and he directs his subject, the technicians, the rare Polaroid Land view camera he has rented for the day with innate directorial control and composure.

With rock music playing in the background, Chuck begins the session by having John Guare, who is dressed in a red-and-white-striped shirt, dark sports jacket, patterned bowtie, black jeans, and white sneakers, sit on a stool in front of the lens. Guare sits up straight. Close begins his instructions:

C.C.: *Okay, John, right into the lens. The critical thing is to hold a position and not rock forward and back. The depth of field is quite critical. In order to get your eyes and your mouth in the same plane, you will have to duck your head in.*

John ducks, and over the course of the next five hours gives the performance of a lifetime as his face changes in emotional increments for each of the twenty Polaroids Close shoots over the course of the session.

At one point Close tells John, who is looking into the camera, that he looks like FDR on the dime. At another point, John gets up from his stool, walks over to the bulletin board where the latest exposure has just been hung to dry, and, reacting with surprise to the thirty-thousand-dollar smile he sees staring back at him, breaks into an unexpected rendition of the Cy Coleman/Dorothy Fields song "Big Spender."

An hour or so of working after the lunch break, Close thinks he has gotten almost enough material. Already he is working out a potential new painting in his mind by staring at the images tacked up on the bulletin board, now full, in the back of the room. John wanders over to Chuck and stares along with him. He asks Chuck about the importance of light in this process, and Chuck replies that it is everything, it defines the form. They go on to talk about other aspects of the work as well, including the stripes in John's shirt, which, Chuck says, become a problem to solve in painting when the pattern of stripes comes up against the "insistent beat of the grid." After one last scan of the images, Chuck wants to get back to work. John pads over to his stool. Chuck swings his wheelchair around, heads toward the camera, and gives his final instructions:

C.C.: *We're going to do one more, John, and then we're done. For this one, give me just the right amount of eyebrow attitude.*

J.G.: *I can make them Nietzchean if you'd like.*

C.C.: *Okay, then. On three. One...two...three.* [Shoots picture.] *Good. Thank you, John.*

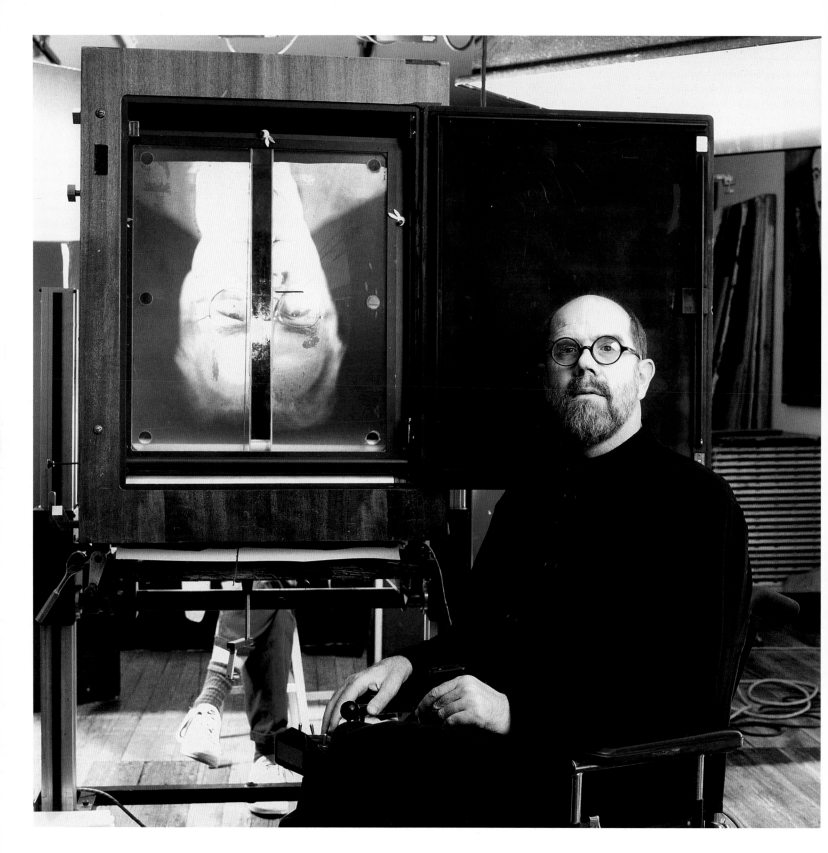

The image of John, who is seated on the other side of the camera, travels through the lens and arrives backward and inverted on the 20 x 24" ground glass focusing screen. When Close achieves the framing and focus he is looking for, the camera is closed. A sandwich of negative, chemicals, and photo paper emerges from the back of the camera. Sixty seconds later the negative is peeled from the positive, and both the artist and the subject immediately assess the results.

J.G.: *Thank you, Chuck.*

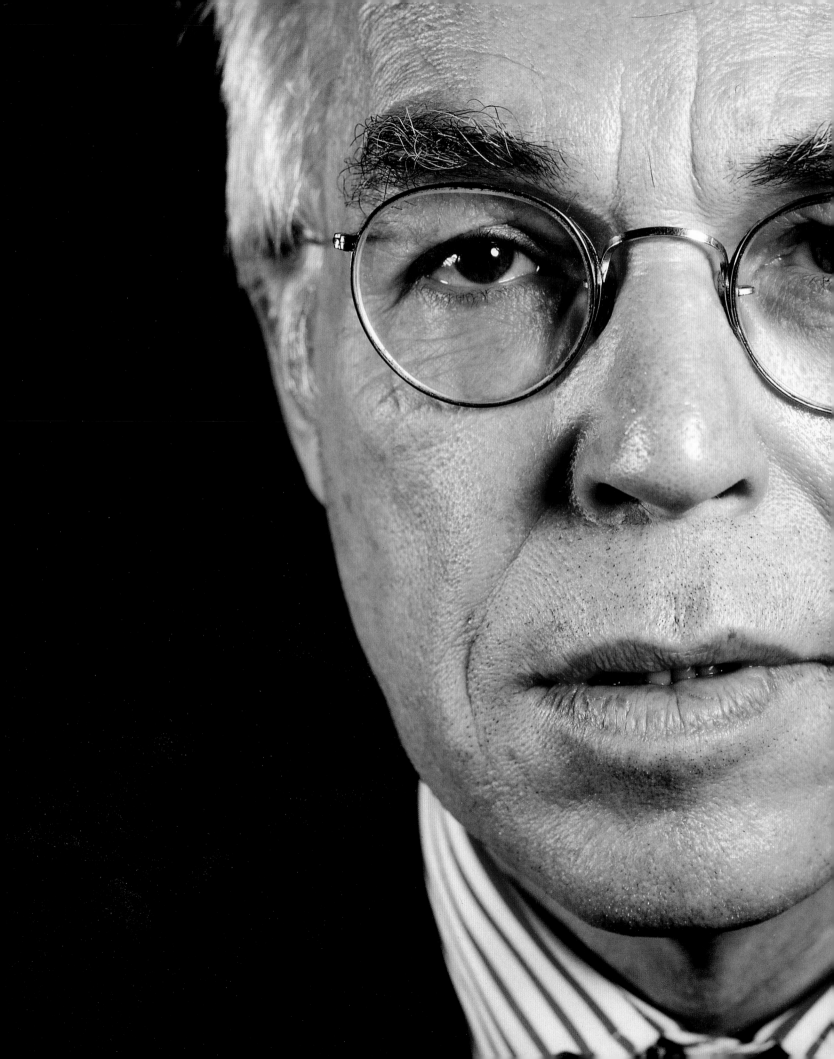

LIST OF SUBJECTS

Chuck Close. JOHN. 1994.
POLAROID PHOTOGRAPH, 20 X 24".
Courtesy Pace/MacGill Gallery, New York

COLLECTION CREDITS

1. Self-Portrait (1986). Collection David Smith
2. Alex (1987). The Toledo Museum of Art, Toledo, Ohio. Gift of The Apollo Society
3 . Lucas I (1986-87). The Metropolitan Museum of Art, Purchase. Lila Acheson Wallace Gift and Gift of Arnold and Milly Glimcher, 1987. (1987.282)
4. Lucas II (1987). Collection Jon and Mary Shirley
5. Self-Portrait (1987). Collection Sidney and George Perutz
6. Francesco I (1987-88). Collection Ron and Ann Pizzuti, Columbus, Ohio
7. Cindy (1988). Private collection
8. Cindy II (1988). Private collection
9. Francesco II. 1988. Collection Arne and Milly Glimcher
10. Alex II (1989). Private collection, New York
11. Elizabeth (1989). Fractional gift of an anonymous donor to The Museum of Modern Art, New York. Photograph © 1995 The Museum of Modern Art, New York
12. Janet (1989). Collection Jon and Mary Shirley
13. Judy (1990). Collection Modern Art Museum of Fort Worth. Gift of Anne Burnett Tandy in Memory of Ollie Lake Burnett, by Exchange
14. Alex (1990). Private collection
15. Bill (1990). Private collection, New York
16. Eric (1990). G.U.C. Collection, Deerfield, Illinois
17. April (1990-91). The Eli and Edythe L. Broad Collection
18. Alex (1991). Collection Lannan Foundation, Los Angeles
19. Bill II (1991). Private collection, New York
20. Lucas (1991). Courtesy Richard Gray Gallery
21. Self-Portrait (1991). Collection PaineWebber Group, Inc., New York
22. Janet (1992). Albright-Knox Art Gallery, Buffalo, New York. George B. and Jenny R. Mathews Fund, 1992
23. John (1992). Collection Michael and Judy Ovitz, Los Angeles
24. Richard (Artschwager) (1992). Private collection
25. Joel (1993). Private collection
26. John II. (1993). Private collection, New York
27. Kiki (1993). Collection Walker Art Center, Minneapolis. Gift of Judy and Kenneth Dayton, 1994
28. Self-Portrait (1993). Private collection
29. Paul (1994). Philadelphia Museum of Art. Purchased with funds from the gift of Mr. and Mrs. Cummins Catherwood, the Edith H. Bell Fund, and with funds contributed by Committee on Twentieth-Century Art
30. Roy I (1994). Courtesy PaceWildenstein, New York
31. Roy II (1994). Courtesy PaceWildenstein, New York
32. Dorothea (1995). Courtesy PaceWildenstein, New York

PHOTOGRAPHY CREDITS

John Back (courtesy PaceWildenstein): pp. 50, 51; Susan Einstein (courtesy Lannan Foundation): p. 78; Bill Jacobson (courtesy PaceWildenstein): Jacket front, front endpaper and details following, half-title spread, pp. 24-25, 36, 56, 57, 63, 64, 68, 69, 76, 79, 80, 81, 85, 87, 88, 89, 91, 93, 95, 99; Copyright © 1995 The Museum of Modern Art, New York: p. 65; Courtesy Pace/MacGill Gallery, New York: pp. 28, 29, 72, 82, 86, 90, 92, 94, 96, 98, 104, 106, 115-122, 124, 126, back jacket; Courtesy PaceWildenstein, New York: pp. 17, 19, 20-21, 28, 29, 37, 39, 40, 52, 53, 54, 55, 58, 62, 66, 67, 70, 71, 73, 74, 75, 77, 83; Copyright © Douglas M. Parker: p. 30; Fred Picker: p. 16; John Reuter (courtesy PaceWildenstein): p. 84; Steven Sloman, New York: p. 35; Ellen Page Wilson (courtesy PaceWildenstein): pp. 50, 51; Bill Zules: pp. 108-114.

ACKNOWLEDGMENTS

The publishers of Yarrow Press would like to thank Chuck Close, John Guare, and the designer Chip Kidd for their inspiring, generous contributions to this book and for the opportunity to work with them.

The publishers are also indebted to Marc Glimcher, Susan Dunn, and Andrea Bundonis at PaceWildenstein; Peter Warner and Laurence Rosenzweig at Thames and Hudson; the photographer Bill Zules; Michael Volonakis; Joe Letitia; Mary Pat Walsh; Cindy Deubel Horowitz; Drew Dunphy; and Robin Zarensky.

A NOTE ON THE TYPE

The text of this book was set in **Bodoni**, a typeface named for Giambattista Bodoni, born in Saluzzo, Piedmont, in 1740. The son of a printer, Bodoni went to Rome as a young man to serve as an apprentice at the press of the Propaganda Fide. In 1768 he was put in charge of the Stamperia Reale in Parma by Duke Ferdinand, a position he held until his death in 1813, in spite of many offers by royal patrons to tempt him elsewhere. His earliest types were those imported from the Paris type foundry of Fournier, but gradually these were superseded by his own designs, which, in the many distinguished books he printed, became famous all over Europe. His later arrangements with the Duke allowed him to print for anyone who would employ him, and with the commissions that flowed in he was able to produce books in French, Russian, German, and English, as well as Italian, Greek, and Latin. His *Manuale Tipographico*, issued in 1818 by his widow, is one of the finest specimen books issued by a printer/type designer.

This book was designed by Chip Kidd, born in Shillington, Pa., in 1964. The son of a chemical engineer, Kidd was sent to Lincoln Park Elementary School as a young man to serve as the star pupil in Miss Cihocki's 5th grade art class. In 1981 he was put in charge of the luggage department of John Wanamaker's department store, a position he held for a number of months, in spite of several offers from the stationary and housewares departments. His earliest designs were those inspired by Detective Comics, but gradually these were superseded by his own designs (while interning at Barash Advertising in State College Pa.), such as the "freshness-seal bag" for Snyder's Potato Chips, which became famous all over Shillington. His later arrangements allowed him to design books for some of the world's most distinguished and talented authors, and to this day, sometimes he just can't believe it. The display type of this book is set in LETTER GOTHIC, designed in 1956 by Roger Robertson.

—C.K., N.Y.C., 1995